How to Build Your Own Web Server

Author: Wes Senter

Table of Contents

Contents

Author: Wes Senter

GREENSCAPELLC.COM

Section 1: How to Build Your Own Web Server

Most of the information that you require is included in this manual and is just a few clicks away!

To save time in the future, print a copy of this document. Choose Print from the File menu, and press Enter to receive all 25 pages of examples and instructions. With the printed document in hand, you are ready to begin the process of learning how to build a web server and manage it for yourself or paying customers.

Introduction

Welcome and thank you for purchasing a copy of our manual. This manual was created as an effort to inform and guide the reader in the operational and technical aspects of building a web server. Once you have read this manual, you should have a good understanding of the "what" and "how" of this material. My name is Wes Senter. I am a Computer Scientist and have been working in this field for over thirty-five years.

About Greenscape Granbury LLC

This document was designed and written by Wes Senter. Wes has over thirty-five years of experience as a Computer Scientist. This manual is very intuitive and simplified for a non-technical person. Of course, it will be to your advantage to have some technical knowledge such as the operation of a computer and a bit about data networking.

The Significance of Hosting Your Own Web Server

I will say this upfront, ladies and gentlemen. Hosting your own webserver is not for the faint hearted. However, maintaining a web server in your home has its advantages and disadvantages.

The advantages of hosting your own server are cost, security, and knowledge. You are going to learn a lot and you will save quite a bit of money.

The main disadvantage of hosting your own server is the lack of redundancy. What I mean by this is that you will most likely have one internet service cable coming into your home from the street. Web hosting providers have several. If one fails, no problem. Data is automatically switched over to one of the good circuits.

To have data circuit failover in your home is possible. Order internet services from two separate companies. Like Charter and AT&T. Purchase a dual port wireless router and you have redundancy.

Is it worth setting up your own Web Server and possibly selling hosting services? My answer is Yes. Just from the knowledge that you gain.

Overview of the Book's Content
We will begin by covering the basics, requirements, and approximate cost to maintain your own web server.

Preparing Readers for the Technical Aspects of Server Setup
If you don't have a technical background, no worries. I will keep you on track with easy to perform instructions. That is the point of purchasing this eBook. I am going to tell you how, step by step.

Understanding Web Servers
The Role of a Web Server is to Basically Perform Two Main Tasks:

Provide DNS services. A web server runs a Nameserver service. The Nameserver communicates with other Nameservers over the internet. It receives and sends DNS records to upstream nameservers, who in turn receives and sends DNS records everywhere.

Eventually, all Nameservers on the internet will have the DNS record for your Webserver. This is how a user sitting in South Africa can access your website. They type in a domain name. That domain name is translated into

6

an IP address by their local Nameserver and then routed to your local Nameserver which sends a request to your local PC.

Provide public access from the internet. This refers to access for websites that view or eCommerce websites that link to PayPal or a credit card processing gateway.

A Note About Credit Card Processing

If you are going to accept credit cards, an SSL certificate is required. Lucky for you, I will show you how to save $75 and get one for free.

7

Web Servers vs. Application Servers

This is good to know, so I included it for you. A web server "serves up" HTML (Hypertext Markup Language) web pages to the public. An application server is typically shared on a LAN (Local Area Network) by locally attached computers in a company setting. This is where most users important files are stored and backed-up to a high-capacity NAS, which stands for "Network Attached Storage".

Overview of Common Web Server Software

Software that you will see after installing your operating system and CWP (Control Web Panel), in this context is all Linux based. Why Linux? Because it is easier to setup and maintain, in comparison to Microsoft Windows IIS servers. Also, 95% of the servers all over the planet are Linux based.

Here are a few of the applications that you will be working with.

Apache: This application is the "traffic cop" for the server. It handles all incoming and outgoing data packets and more. I won't go into detail here as this is not within the scope of this tutorial.

CSF: Config Server Firewall: This application is not part of the Linux O/S. It is a 3rd party firewall that is excellent. You do not want to run a web server without it. Once you get your server up and running, I will tell you how to view in real time, the log file. Here, you can quickly see how many hackers are "hammering" your

server, looking for a weakness. Most are from China, Russia, Vietnam, and the U.S.A. CSF will monitor the Linux log file and when it sees incoming data packets from the same IP address (we will discuss IP addresses later) hitting your server over and over, it will automatically block those addresses.

8

CWP: Control Web Panel: This application makes the management and setup of your web server a piece of cake. It is a free, easy to use control panel for servers and VPS. No more cryptic Lunix commands. The CSF firewall is already included. It is one of the top firewalls in the industry for web servers. CWP contains a modern, attractive interface. 35,000 servers run CWP. There is an upgrade to CWP Pro if you wish for only $12.00 per year. CWP Pro unlocks many of the features that are locked in the free version. If you plan on using HTTPS Certificates on your domain names (highly recommended), you should spend $12.00 and upgrade. It is worth it.

CWP is a complete management system for Linux. It replaces the cryptic command set with a very nice menu driven system that is easy to use. It allows complete control of most major services running on the Centos Server.

After successfully entering the panel, you should see something like:

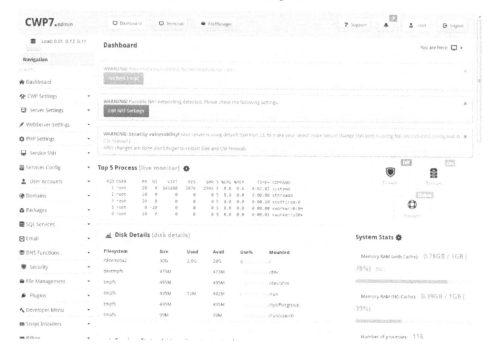

Section 2: Selecting the Hardware

Hardware Considerations

The Webserver is not the only piece of equipment you need to consider. In addition to the webserver, you will need a large UPS (Un-Interruptible Power Supply). You will also need a fast internet connection with a "dedicated IP address". If you ask your Internet Service Provider for one, they can typically issue that to you. That will be covered in the CWP section. A word of advice from someone (me) who use to design networks for the U.S. and foreign governments. If you are going to sell services on this web server, install a fail-over network path. I have Spectrum and I would not even attempt to host a web server, using their internet service.

10

Contact another carrier in your area and have them also install their internet service. Order the service with only their modem. No wireless router with ports on it. Then order a dual-wan-port router and replace the one you have. This way, if Spectrum or AT&T's service fails, as an example, the router will still have connectivity to the other carrier.

If you do this, don't forget to open up the internal network ports in your new router. If you forgot the ports, just refer to the end of this eBook where they are all shown.

Available Servers

If you need a Linux server for your business, we offer an alternative to building it yourself. Food for thought.

Our Servers are custom built using the highest quality parts that money can buy. Sounds expensive? Nope. We build them in our shop with little overhead. These can be viewed on our website: https://greenscapellc.com. These servers are fully configured and ready to connect to the net. We will help you get up and running at no charge. One of our systems is shown below.

This is one of our best servers. It is a custom-built Intel I-9 with 16 GB of RAM (Plenty RAM for Linux). It runs at almost 5.3 Ghz. non-stop. How, without overheating? If you notice the custom water-cooling system. If you also notice the temperature and flow gauge, it shows the coolant temperature at 84 degrees Fahrenheit. CPUs can run much faster if kept cool as they tend to overheat when overclocked. Heat is the enemy, so we provide high-performance, water-cooled processors.

It also has fast M.2 memory installed directly on the bus, so it reads and writes data much faster. This system will boot in under five seconds.

Note that the system shown cannot be shipped due to the fragile acrylic tubing seen. We substitute a water-cooling system that can be shipped. It uses black silicone wrapped tubing. This can be viewed on our website.

View the Details

Go to https://greenscapellc.com

Section 3: Building and Configuring a Web Server

Hardware and Software Requirements

What you will need to complete the installation of Linux Centos 7 and Control Web Panel is shown below.

The Server - A computer system that has at least one I-5 Intel processor. An I-7 or I-9 would be better. The system should have at least 16 GB of RAM and a network interface card that will run at 100 MBps. 1 GBps would be better. Don't purchase a proprietary computer system. When you start adding paying customers, you will have to add memory. Proprietary systems RAM cost double what you would pay if you purchased a custom-built system. Last, but not least, our servers come with dual 2.5GBps ports for connectivity to the internet.

The Router – Obtain a router that has a minimum of 1 GBps ports. That will be compatible with your server should you have a 1 GBps network card installed. Use CAT 6E cabling from the router to the server or fiber-optic if your router and server supports it. You can always purchase an adapter to convert Ethernet to Fiber.

Internet Speed – Go as fast as you can afford. Many ISPs today offer 1GBps fiber optic connectivity. If you are planning on hosting other people's websites, I would most highly recommend this. A 1GBps service will handle upwards of 100 users.

Your Firewall – I would recommend you research this. The better the firewall, the less likely you will be hacked on your local network. The firewall on the server, "CSF" is one of the best in the industry so it is highly unlikely you will be hacked. There is also a 3rd party service called "Bit Ninja" that is second to none. Just give them your servers IP address and they will stop Chinese, Russians, and others before they

13

ever get to your server. Their monthly fee is only $20.00. The IP address you will give them is not your local network address (192.168.1.X). It is the IP address the ISP (Internet Service Provider) gave you. You can easily get it by running your browser and going to whatismyipaddress.com.

A Memory Stick (USB) – This is a requirement for the installation of Centos. You will need to build a bootable Centos memory stick to start the installation to your server. Your memory stick should be at least 30GB. We will help you with that in coming chapters.

Installation

The scope of this tutorial covers the installation and configuration of a Linux Centos based web server. Windows servers are not addressed. So, we have come to the meat of this eBook. We now get to start having fun.

Centos 7

Follow the Steps Below

Prior to the installation, ensure that you have a working and preferably fast internet connection. The Centos installation requires an internet connection.

First Things First

You will need to create a bootable memory stick. So, if you don't have one, purchase one that has at least 30 GB of memory.

Use your browser and go to Centos.org using the link below. https://centos.org. Click Download in the top menu. The download page will appear.

Click x86_64 on the first line. You will now be presented with all the downloads that are available. Click the first URL, http://mirror.vacares.com/centos/7.9.2009/isos/x86_64/. On the next page, click the first URL, CentOS-7-x86_64-DVD-..>. This download will show up in your Windows Downloads folder in a couple of hours. To check the progress, click on the circle with a down pointed arrow in the top bar of the browser. Once you open the download icon, do not click on the file being downloaded.

Once the image is downloaded, we need to make sure the memory stick is bootable, and we have transferred Centos to it. Download balenaEtcher at balenaetcher.org and download the latest version for Windows. Run the installation.

Run balenaetcher by clicking the icon that should now be on your desktop. Click Flash from file. Next, click Select Target and choose the Centos file in your download's directory. Then, click Flash! This will take about 10 minutes.

Setting the BIOS:

Take the memory stick and plug it into the system you are using as the server. If you are using the same system, reboot it and press the "F2" and "F10" keys sequentially over and over. On most motherboards, this will put you into the BIOS panel. When in the BIOS panel, go to the BOOT panel and change the boot sequence to boot from the memory stick first. Save and exit.

Centos Installation

The Centos configuration panel should appear.

First, select the language that you want. Click Continue.

Next, click Date and Time. Set it. Don't overlook the time and date on the bottom bar. Click Done.

15

Click Installation Destination. Click the Drive that you wish to install Centos on. If you have two drives, click them both. Click Done. If you get an error that says you don't have enough disk space, click the reclaim space button. In the panel that appears, you should see your memory stick and the original drive. Make sure you do not delete space from the memory stick. Move the cursor down to the original drive and click the Delete button. DO NOT CLICK THE DELETE ALL Button! Click the Reclaim Space Button.

Click, Network and Hostname. Click the Configure button. In the top bar, click the IPv4 Settings TAB. Click the ADD button.

Enter your IP address for the server under the Address column. If you did not get a dedicated IP from your ISP, let's use a temporary one. If you most likely have a wireless router, it's default IP address is 192.168.1.1. So let's try and use 192.168.1.57. So, type that address into the Address space. Next, under the Netmask column space, type 255.255.255.0. In the Gateway space, type 192.168.1.1 . Now, under Additional DNS Servers, type in 8.8.8.8. Check the box that asks "Require IPv4 addressing". Click the SAVE button.

On the Network and Host Name panel, click the OFF slider in the top right corner of the screen. Make sure that you see "Connected" under the wall plug icon in the middle of the screen. Click DONE.

Click "Software Selection". Click "Minimal Install" and then click DONE.

Click "Root Password". Enter a password and Click Done. Click new user. Enter the ID and password. Click Done.

The installer will run for a while. After it completes, remove the memory stick from the server and click the Reboot Button.

"CWP" – Control Web Panel Installation

Now that Linux Centos is running on your server, it's time to install CWP and configure it.

Login to your server. Use root as the login ID and the password you defined during the Centos installation. At the prompt, enter the following commands.

Yum Update -y: #yum update -y. This command will download all updates and install them automatically.

Yum Install Wget: #yum install wget. This command installs the Wget Utility. Used for downloading and installing utilities.

Change the Directory: #cd /usr/local/src/

Download the latest version of CWP: #wget http://centos-webpanel.com/cwp-el7-latest .

Start the CWP Installation: #sh cwp-el7-latest.

This installation may take an hour to complete the installation because it must compile Apache and PHP from source code.

When the installation is complete, you will see a message to Press Enter for server reboot: Press Enter.

Access CWP by using a browser on a different computer and entering http://192.168.x.x:2031 and use your root password.

You notice we are using your local IP address. This is because you can't access your new server from the internet yet. That must be set up. Do you remember how to get your local IP address?

Section 4: Configuration

Simply follow this step-by-step guide for configuring CWP on your Linux Server. The scope of this tutorial covers the configuration of a Linux based web server. You have already installed CWP.

1. **Set up Root Email:** This is important for notifications. Click the Set Root Email button. Change the default email address from my@email.com to your original email address.

   If you wish, you can also set an email address for CSF/LFD Firewall alerts. Click Save Changes button at bottom of the screen. You can return to this Settings page at any time by clicking Go to CWP Settings and Edit Settings from the menu to the left.

2. **Set Up Hosting Plans:** These are web hosting packages you usually see on many hosting providers. Generally, you can sell different web hosting packages for different prices.

3. Go to Packages then click Packages from the left sidebar menu.

4. You'll notice the default package already there. You can simply modify it or create your own package(s).

5. Click Add New Package button, the green one on the top right corner. Fill in all required fields as you wish. Click the Create button once you are finished.

6. **Account Type:** you can choose either General or Reseller. A reseller account can create child user accounts. Choose General if you plan to use CWP as your personal web hosting server.

Setup NAT

What is NAT? NAT stands for "**Network Address Translation**". It is a technology used in networking to map private IP addresses to a single public IP address. It's commonly employed in home and business networks to enable multiple devices with private IP addresses to share a single public IP address for accessing resources on the internet. NAT serves several essential purposes:

1. **Conservation of Public IP Addresses:** With the depletion of IPv4 addresses, NAT allows multiple devices in a local network to use private IP addresses that aren't routable on the public internet. Only one public IP address is needed for the entire local network.
2. **Security:** NAT provides a level of security by acting as a barrier between the local network and the internet. External entities on the internet can't directly initiate connections to devices with private IP addresses, as the NAT device typically doesn't forward incoming connections unless explicitly configured to do so.
3. **Load Balancing:** In some cases, NAT devices can perform basic load balancing by distributing incoming requests to

   different devices in the local network based on port numbers. This can help distribute the load among multiple servers or services.

   NAT works by maintaining a translation table that keeps track of the correspondence between private IP addresses and ports and the single public IP address and ports. When a device in the local network sends a request to a server on the internet, the NAT device modifies the source IP address and port in the packet header to its own public IP address and a unique port number. When the server sends the response back to the NAT device, it uses the information in the translation table to forward the response to the appropriate device in the local network.

4. **Setting Up NAT on CWP:** In the CWP home panel, go to "Edit Settings". Enter the shared IP address to be used for sharing the public IP address. Scroll down and click on activate NAT-ed network

configuration checkbox. Click "Save Changes". Return to the Dashboard and restart CWP services and Apache services.

NAT is now set up on your server. It will handle the IP address translation between the local IP address for the server and the external public IP address supplied by your ISP (Internet Service Provider).

As long as your port definitions are correctly set up in your broadband router, everything should work. See the setup instructions for your home router on page 24.

Setup the Nameservers

Next, you will configure your nameservers. A nameserver is a computer that runs DNS or Domain Name Services. DNS works hand in hand with Apache to route data packets to their final destination. And, to receive the packets.

DNS primarily assigns IP addresses to words, such as your domain name. When you type in https://google.com or https://www.google.com , your DNS server has the IP address to google.com stored and knows where to send it. That is very simplified and is beyond the scope of this manual.

Select DNS Functions >> Edit Nameserver IPS:

1. Change the default Nameservers from NS1 and NS2.centos-webpanel.com to your own. Make sure both checkboxes at the bottom are checked. Click Save Changes.
2. The common format to use is ns1 and ns2.yourdomainname.com. Next, you will need to go to your domain name registrar. For example, GoDaddy. Find your domain name in your product list. Click DNS for your domain name.
3. On the DNS Management page, click Hostnames.
4. Enter ns1 and n2 under Host Column, then enter the Ip address for both under the IP Addresses Column. Click Save.
5. Next, click Nameservers in the top menu and change from GoDaddy's nameservers to your own. For your name servers, enter ns1.yourdomain.com and ns2.yourdomain.com and save.

6. You will need to wait at least an hour before your domain names have propagated the internet.

Setup the Webserver

A webserver is the main service used to handle web requests. Apache, Nginx, and Lightspeed are ready to use.

Go to Web Server Settings and choose Select Webserver from the left sidebar menu.

Leave the default configuration, Apache. Click the Save and Rebuild button.

Choose the PHP Version

Depending on your website's needs, you may need to choose a specific PHP version.

Go to PHP Settings and select PHP Version Switcher. I would recommend changing the PHP version from v5.6.x to v7.4.x. Click Save Build. After selecting the desired PHP version, CWP will start the PHP compiler. Installation can take up to **10 minutes.**

Securing the Server

This step is critical. Without your firewall running, you will be hacked, period! The security applications are the most important applications to be configured. Perform the following.

From the menu, go to Security >> Firewall Manager. See the image below.

Click the Enable Firewall button. Exit and return to the same panel shown above and make sure the button to the right of Firewall manager shows "Firewall is Enabled".

For extra security, look at **bitninja.com.** They are a 3rd party service that provides intrusion prevention. All you must do is give them your servers IP address. They will weed out all the hackers before they ever get to your server. So, you will have two layers of firewalls. I have been running this configuration for three years and have never been hacked. Not once, although hackers hit my server constantly.

SSH Security

The minute you are up and running on the internet, your new server becomes a soft target for hackers trying to gain access to SSH. For this reason, I advise hardening SSH security first.

So, what is SSH? It is a network protocol that allows you to connect to remote servers. It ensures the secure transfer of data between two computers. This may be the way you will need to connect to your new server for administration.

What is the SSH Client? The SSH Client runs on your PC, unlike SSH that runs on your server. My favorite SSH client application is called "Putty". It has been around for a long time. It is simple to use and not buggy.

What we will do to **harden your new server** is to change the SSH default port. Hackers love to hammer this port so they can gain access to your server. TCP port 22 is the standard port for SSH. Let's change that to port 2520.

Changing the SSH Port in CWP

Login to CWP using root and your password. Goto Security > CSF Firewall. Click Firewall Configuration.

Be very careful what you change in here!

1. Scroll down to "Allow incoming TCP ports."
2. On the TCP_IN line, delete 22. Then, go to the end of the line and insert 2520. Be sure and enter a comma between 2096 and 2520 and close the quotes.
3. Scroll down to "Allow outgoing TCP ports."
4. On the TCP_OUT line, delete 22. Then, go to the end of the line and insert 2520. Be sure and enter a comma between 2443 and 2520 and close the quotes.
5. Scroll down until you see the same entries again except, they show TCP6_IN and TCP6_OUT. Make the same changes here.
6. Save the changes by clicking the button at the bottom.

23

7. Now go to Services Config > SSH Configuration.
8. This will open the SSH config file.
9. Look for the line: #Port 22
10. Chage 22 to 2520 and remove the # character so it looks like Port 2520.
11. Click the Save Changes button at the bottom.
12. Return to the Dashboard and scroll down to Services Status.
13. Find the SSH Server. Click Restart.
14. You should see a popup window that shows "SSH Server Successfully Restarted".
15. Now, go to Security > CSF Firewall and click the Firewall Quick Restart Button.

Create User Accounts

Create your first user account. You can use this account for your own or for your client.

1. Go to User Accounts and click New Account.
2. This option will create a new user and a MySQL account with the same credentials.
3. Fill in all required fields such as Domain Name, Username, and the Password will be automatically generated. By default, shell access should be disabled.
4. Click the Create button once you are finished.

Login to User Panel and Install Free SSL Certificate

Login to CWP user panel at http://x.x.x.x:2082 or https://x.x.x.x:2083 if you already have an SSL certificate installed. **Note that you must upgrade to CWPro to be able to use the AutoSSL feature.

a. If you do not have an SSL certificate: Use
   http://yourdomain.com:2082

b. If you do have an SSL certificate: Use
   https://yourdomain.com:2083

c. Click **Domains** and select **AutoSSL (Pro Version Only)**. I
   would recommend purchasing CWP Pro. It is only $10 per
   year.

   Choose the domain name that you want to install the SSL
   certificate on. Also, check **Mail, Webmail, and Ftp**. Click
   the **Install** Button. The SSL certificate is generated and
   installed in an instant.

d. **Note:** You can issue a free AutoSSL certificate for any
   website on your server. Here is how. First, upgrade to
   CWPro.

e. Login to **CWP Administrator GUI dashboard** at
   http://x.x.x.x:2030 or https://x.x.x.x:2031 if you already
   have an SSL certificate installed.

f. Go to **Webserver Settings** and click **SSL Certificates**.

g. Now, click the **AutoSSL [FREE] tab** to reveal all the
   options.

h. Find the domain you want and check the services boxes to
   make the SSL certificate available to those services. I
   would recommend Webmail and Ftp.

i. Click **the Install SSL button**. ** Only in the Pro Edition.

j. Click the List Installed Tab to view the new SSL
   certificate.

SEE the image shown below.

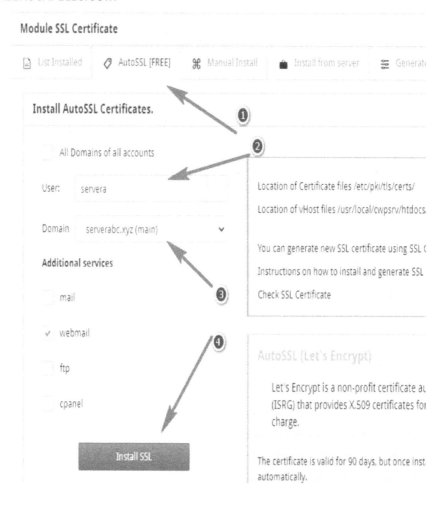

Setting Up for FTP

This procedure will show you how to setup FTP so you can upload your webpages to your new server. I have another book titled "How to Create Your Own Website using HTML5, PHP, and MySQL". It will be available very soon.

    a. Download "FileZilla". This is a very good FTP program for Windows 10.
    b. After it downloads, double click the .exe file and install it.
    c. After the install completes, run the application.
    d. When FileZilla loads, the window is laid out with your local files on the left and the server files on the right (after you connect to the server).
    e. In the top menu bar, click File > Site Manager.
    f. Click the New Site Button. Enter your website name where it shows New Site.
    g. On the right side, for Host, enter your domain name. For Protocol, enter FTP – File Transfer Protocol. For Encryption, enter Use Explicit FTP over TLS if available. Login Type is Normal. For User, enter the name you setup for FTP in the control panel. For Password, enter the password you setup in the control panel. Click OK.
    h. Don't panic. We have not yet set up FTP on the server side yet. Let's do that now.

From the main CWP panel, select File Management. Then click FTP Manager v2. Click "Add User" TAB. Select the domain name. Enter a username and password. Leave the path alone and click Submit.

That's it. At this point, go to FileZilla. Go back to File > Site Manager and check to make sure the username and password you just created for FTP on the server matches what you have in User: and Password: Click Connect. When the certificate appears, check the box "Always trust certificate in future sessions". Click OK.

Now, when FTP connects, you will only see a Skelton web site on the right side of the screen. That is the server. On the left side, browse to find your website's folder and click it. Now, you should see all your web files in the folder. As you build your website, drag, and drop the file name from the left side of the screen to the right side. You are done!

Bringing It All Together

For every new user, you will need to perform the following:

1. Go to User Accounts > New Account
   Complete the Form.
   Save.

2. Go to Email > Email Accounts
   Click the Add New Domain Mail button.
   Select the User from the Drop-Down Box.

3. Enter an address (Just the first part, before the @ sign).
   Enter the passwords.
   Click Create Mail

   Login to CWP user panel at http://x.x.x.x:2082
   Use the public IP address or a domain name associated with the public address followed by "/cwp". To login locally, use the local IP address assigned to the account followed by "/cwp".

   Once logged in to a new account, if you want AutoSSL and the Website Builder to work, you must upgrade to CWPro. It is only $12 per year. I do not get any kickbacks / commissions for any referrals in the book.

Thank you so much for purchasing my eBook. Be on the lookout for How to Build Your Own Website Using HTML5/PHP/MySQL

Having Trouble Connecting to the Internet?

This section is for the home user whose server is connected to a broadband router with ethernet ports. Have you connected your server to one of these?

If you have, you will most likely need to set up port routing in your router. Here is the problem. Traffic from your server sends data packets outbound with no problem. However, one of your routers' primary functions is to act as a firewall.

Taking that into account, your ports are being blocked by your router and never make it to the server. So, follow the instructions below. I use a Netgear Nighthawk XR500. However, all routers have the same basic configuration options.

1. Using your browser, go to 192.168.1.1 (Default IP Address for most routers.
2. When the main screen comes up, go to Settings > Advanced.
3. Click Port Forwarding. This is where you define your inbound ports and where the data packets are sent to your local network.
4. Click "Add Custom Service". For Service Name enter "DNS". Leave the Protocol as is. Check the box "Use the same port range for Internal port."
5. For "External port range" enter 53. Then, for internal network IP address (your server), enter the IP address. Click "Apply".
6. Repeat the above procedure for CWP (2082-2083). Type the ports in exactly as shown.
7. Next, do the same procedure for CWP. (Port 2031)
8. Next, do the same for HTTPS. (Port 443)
9. Finally, do the same for FTP. (Ports 20-21)
10. Don't forget to click "Apply" for each port you add.

You can check to see if your DNS server is talking to the internet by going to www.intodns.com. Enter your domain name and it will tell you the status of it.

Greenscape Granbury LLC
Wes Senter

Section 5: About the Author

The author of "How to Build Your Own Webserver" is Wes Senter. Wes is a Computer Scientist, trained as a Network Engineer by the U.S. Air Force. He has over thirty-five years of experience in Information Technology. He is both Cisco and Microsoft Certified (CCNA, MCSE). His fields of expertise are listed below.

- Network Engineering
- Network Management
- Network Architecture
- Applications Design
- Applications Authoring
- Web Design
- Web Programming
- IBM Systems Programming
- IBM SNAP/D
- Technical Documentation
- Technical Diagramming
- eBook Authoring
- Music Producer
- Country Music Artist

References

CWP Control Panel. *Control-Web Panel Documentation*.Control-Webpanel.com

LINANTO LLC. *Control-Web Panel Documentation*. 0160 Tbilisi, Pekin Avenue N44 GEORGIA

GREENSCAPELLC.COM
Greenscape Granbury LLC (2023). *How To Build Your Own Web Server*. 3724 Cove Timber Ave. Granbury, TX 76049